Congressional
Research
Service

The United States as a Net Debtor Nation: Overview of the International Investment Position

James K. Jackson
Specialist in International Trade and Finance

November 8, 2012

Congressional Research Service
7-5700
www.crs.gov
RL32964

Summary

The international investment position of the United States is an annual measure of the assets Americans own abroad and the assets foreigners own in the United States. The net position, or the difference between the two, sometimes is referred to as a measure of U.S. international indebtedness. This designation is not strictly correct, because the net international investment position reveals the difference between the total assets Americans own abroad and the total amount of assets foreigners own in the United States. These assets generate flows of capital into and out of the economy that have important implications for the value of the dollar in international exchange markets. Some Members of Congress and some in the public have expressed concerns about the U.S. net international investment position because of the role foreign investors are playing in U.S. capital markets and the potential for large outflows of income and services payments. Some observers also argue that the U.S. reliance on foreign capital inflows places the economy in a vulnerable position.

Contents

Background 1

Valuing Investments 3

Investment Patterns 6

International Investment: Sources and Economic Impact 12

Congressional Response 17

Figures

Figure 1. U.S. Direct Investment Abroad:
   Estimated Value of Accumulated Position, 1990-2011 5

Figure 2. Foreign Direct Investment in the United States:
   Estimated Value of Accumulated Position, 1990-2011 6

Figure 3. U.S.-Owned Assets Abroad and Foreign–Owned Assets in the United States,
   1994-2011 8

Figure 4. Foreign Official and Private Investment Positions in the United States, 1994-
   2011 10

Figure 5. U.S. and Foreign Investment Position, By Major Component, 2011 11

Figure 6. U.S. Income Receipts and Payments on U.S.-Owned Assets Abroad and on
   Foreign-Owned Assets in the United States, 2011 15

Tables

Table 1. U.S. Net International Investment Position 1

Table 2. U.S. International Investment Status 8

Table 3. Saving and Investment in Selected Countries and Areas; 2007-2011, and 2012 13

Table 4. Estimates of Wealth in the United States, 2011 Current-Cost, Gross Stock Values 16

Contacts

Author Contact Information 18

Background

The U.S. international investment position represents the accumulated nominal value of U.S.-owned assets abroad and foreign-owned assets in the United States measured on an annual basis at the end of the calendar year. Some observers refer to the net of this investment position (or the difference between the value of U.S.-owned assets abroad and the value of foreign-owned assets in the United States) as a debt, or that it indicates that the United States is in a net debtor position, because the value of foreign-owned assets in the United States is greater than the value of U.S.-owned assets abroad. In fact, the nation's international investment position is not a measure of the nation's indebtedness similar to the debt borrowed by some developing countries, but it is an accounting of assets. By year-end 2011, the latest year for which data are available, the overseas assets of U.S. residents totaled approximately $21 trillion, while foreigners had acquired about $25 trillion in assets in the United States, with direct investment measured at historical cost. As a result, the U.S. net international investment position was about $4.2 trillion in the negative with direct investment measured at historical cost, as indicated in **Table 1**.

Table 1. U.S. Net International Investment Position

(in billions of dollars)

Type of Investment	2008	2008	2010	2011
Net international investment position of the United States:				
With direct investment at current cost	$-3,260.2	$-2,321.8	$-2,473.6	$-4,030.3
With direct investment at market value	-3,995.3	-2,661.3	-2,813.4	-4,812.4
With direct investment at historical cost	-3,425.4	-2,503.8	-2,656.2	-4,195.3
Financial derivatives	159.6	126.3	110.4	126.3
U.S.-owned assets abroad:				
With direct investment at current cost	19,464.7	18,511.7	20,298.4	21,132.4
With direct investment at market value	18,818.6	18,769.4	20,758.3	20,950.8
With direct investment at historical cost	18,948.7	18,000.9	19,782.5	20,606.4
Financial derivatives	6,127.5	3,489.8	3,652.3	4,704.7
U.S. official reserve assets	293.7	403.8	488.7	536.0
U.S. Government assets, other	624.1	82.8	75.2	178.9
U.S. private assets:				
With direct investment at current cost	12,419.4	14,535.3	16,082.2	15,712.8
With direct investment at market value	11,773.3	14,793.1	16,542.1	15,531.2
With direct investment at historical cost	11,903.4	14,024.5	15,566.3	15,186.7
Direct investment abroad:				
—At current cost	3,748.5	4,029.5	4,306.8	4,681.6
—At market value	3,102.4	4,287.2	4,766.7	4,500.0
—At historical cost	3,232.5	3,518.7	3,790.9	4,155.6
Foreign securities	3,985.7	5,565.6	6,336.4	5,922.0
—Bonds	1,237.3	1,570.3	1,689.5	1,763.8

Type of Investment	2008	2008	2010	2011
—Corporate stocks	2,748.4	3,995.3	4,646.9	4,158.2
U.S. claims by US nonbanking concerns	930.9	930.3	874.8	796.8
U.S. claims reported by US banks	3,754.3	4,009.9	4,564.2	4,312.4
Foreign-owned assets in the United States:				
With direct investment at current cost	22,724.9	20,833.5	22,772.0	25,162.6
With direct investment at market value	22,813.9	21,430.7	23,571.7	25,763.2
With direct investment at historical cost	22,374.1	20,504.7	22,438.7	24,801.7
Financial derivatives	5,967.8	3,363.4	3,541.9	4,578.4
Foreign official assets in the United States	3,943.9	4,402.8	4,912.7	5,250.8
Foreign private assets:				
With direct investment at current cost	12,813.2	13,067.2	14,317.4	15,333.4
With direct investment at market value	12,902.2	13,664.5	15,117.1	15,934.0
With direct investment at historical cost	12,462.5	12,738.4	13,984.0	14,972.5
Direct investment in the United States:				
—At current cost	2,397.4	2,398.2	2,597.7	2,908.8
—At market value	2,486.4	2,995.5	3,397.4	3,509.4
—At historical cost	2,046.7	2,069.4	2,264.4	2,547.8
U.S. Treasury securities	852.5	791.0	1,101.8	1,418.1
U.S. other securities	4,620.7	5,319.9	5,934.0	5,968.2
—Corporate and other bonds	2,770.6	2,825.6	2,915.7	2,910.0
—Corporate stocks	1,850.1	2,494.3	3,018.3	3,058.2
U.S. currency	301.1	313.8	342.1	397.1
U.S. liabilities by U.S. nonbanking concerns	740.6	706.4	643.6	629.7
U.S. liabilities reported by U.S. banks	3,901.0	3,537.9	3,698.2	4,011.6

Source: Nguyen, Elena L., The International Investment Position of the United States at Yearend 2011, Survey of Current Business, July 2012. p. 18.

Foreign investors who acquire U.S. assets do so at their own risk and accept the returns accordingly, unlike the debt owed by developing countries where debt service payments are guaranteed in advance. The returns on the assets in the investment position, except for bonds, are not guaranteed, and foreign investors gain or lose in the same way as U.S. domestic investors. As **Table 1** indicates, these investments include such financial assets as corporate stocks and bonds, government securities, and direct investment[1] in businesses and real estate. The value of these

[1] The United States defines foreign direct investment as the ownership or control, directly or indirectly, by one foreign person (individual, branch, partnership, association, government, etc.) of 10% or more of the voting securities of an incorporated U.S. business enterprise or an equivalent interest in an unincorporated U.S. business enterprise. 15 CFR § 806.15 (a)(1). Similarly, the United States defines direct investment abroad as the ownership or control, directly or indirectly, by one person (individual, branch, partnership, association, government, etc.) of 10% or more of the voting securities of an incorporated business enterprise or an equivalent interest in an unincorporated business enterprise. 15 (continued...)

assets, measured on an annual basis, can change as a result of purchases and sales of new or existing assets; changes in the financial value of the assets that arise through appreciation, depreciation, or inflation; changes in the market values of stocks and bonds; or changes in the value of currencies. The change in the net international investment position between 2010 and 2011 arises from a net decrease in the value of U.S. private assets owned abroad as a result of a large revaluation downward in the values of corporate stocks owned abroad by U.S. entities and other private investments that was larger than the value of new private investments abroad and an increase in net foreign investment in U.S. assets coupled with a upward revaluation of assets in the United States owned by foreigners. The Department of Commerce also uses three different methods for valuing direct investments that yield roughly comparable estimates for the net position, although the three methods do provide estimates on U.S. direct investment abroad and foreign direct investment that have varied considerably at times. Unless otherwise indicated, this report uses direct investment valued as historical cost.

Valuing Investments

The Department of Commerce provides updated estimates on the nation's international investment position each year, typically in July, based on data for the previous year through the end of the calendar year. Except for direct investment, all of the accounts in the international investment position are estimated directly by the Department of Commerce's Bureau of Economic Analysis (BEA) relative to readily observable market prices. For example, the value of positions in portfolio investments (securities), gold, loans, currencies, and bank deposits can be directly estimated by the BEA based on the face values or market prices of recent transactions. The Department of Commerce does not attempt to deflate the annual nominal amounts for direct investment with a specific price deflator. Instead, the Department publishes alternative estimates of direct investment based on current cost, market value, and historical cost to provide other measures of the value of direct investment.

Estimating the value of direct investments, however, presents a number of challenges. According to the Department of Commerce, these challenges arise because foreign direct investments, "typically represent illiquid ownership interests in companies that may possess many unique attributes—such as customer base, management, and ownership of intangible assets—whose values in the current period are difficult to determine, because there is no widely accepted standard for revaluing company financial statements at historical cost into prices of the current period."[2]

As a result, the Department of Commerce estimates the U.S. international investment position in three ways, reflecting three different accounting methods for estimating the value of direct investments: historical cost; current cost; and market value. Initially, direct investments are valued at historical cost, or the cost at the time of the investment. This historical cost value can become outdated because it is not updated to account for changes in the value of an investment through appreciation, or through internal growth and expansion, or through changes in various intangible assets. The current cost approach estimates the value of capital equipment and land at

(...continued)

CFR § 806.15 (a)(1).

[2] Nguyen, Elena L., "The International Investment Position of the United States at Yearend 2011," *Survey of Current Business*, July 2012, p. 18.

their current replacement cost using general cost indexes, and inventories, using estimates of their replacement cost, rather than at their historical cost. The third measure, market value, uses indexes of stock market prices to revalue the owners' equity share of direct investment.

For the most part, the current cost and historical cost estimates have tracked closely together for U.S. direct investment abroad and for foreign direct investment in the United States, as indicated in **Figure 1** and **Figure 2**, respectively. These two measures of direct investment demonstrate a steady increase in the value of the investments over the 21-year period from 1990 to 2011. The market value estimate of direct investment, however, displays a markedly different pattern. These estimates spiked during the rapid runup in stock market values in the 1990s and then dropped sharply when market values declined at the end of the 1990s. The market value estimates rose sharply again in 2003 through 2007, as the rebound in stock market values pushed up the estimated market value of firms. The data for 2008, however, offer one clear indication of the economic recession that began affecting the U.S. economy in 2008 and the initial stages of the financial crisis that negatively affected stock market indexes in nearly all markets.

In 2008, the market value of U.S. direct investment position abroad, or the cumulative amount of such investment, fell by 41% and the value of foreign direct investment position in the United States fell by 30%, while direct investment valued at current cost or historical cost registered slight positive gains in nominal terms. In contrast, the market value of U.S. direct investment abroad rose by 38% in 2009 from $3.1 trillion to $4.3 trillion and the market value of foreign direct investment in the United States rose by 22% from $2.5 trillion to $3.0 trillion. During the same period, however, the value of U.S. direct investment abroad rose by 8.5% and 9.7% in terms of current cost and historical cost, respectively. Similarly, the value of foreign corporate stocks owned by U.S. investors rose by 37% from $4.0 trillion in 2008 to $5.5 trillion in 2009. In comparison, the value of U.S. corporate stocks owned by foreign investors rose by 14% from $4.6 trillion in 2008 to $5.3 trillion in 2009. In 2010, the U.S. direct investment position abroad increased by 10% valued at historical cost, 11.8% valued in market value terms, and 8.9% in current value terms. In addition, in 2010, the foreign direct investment position in the United States increased by 10.8% (historical cost), 14.0% (market value), and 8.9% (current cost). In 2011, U.S. direct investment abroad valued at historical cost and current cost rose by 9.6% and 8.7%, respectively, while the value of such investments fell by 5.6% in terms of market value, reflecting the fall in stock market values overall in Europe and elsewhere. Also, during 2011 foreign direct investment in the United States rose by 13.5% in historical cost terms, by 12% in current cost terms, and by 3.3% in market value terms.

**Figure 1. U.S. Direct Investment Abroad:
Estimated Value of Accumulated Position, 1990-2011**

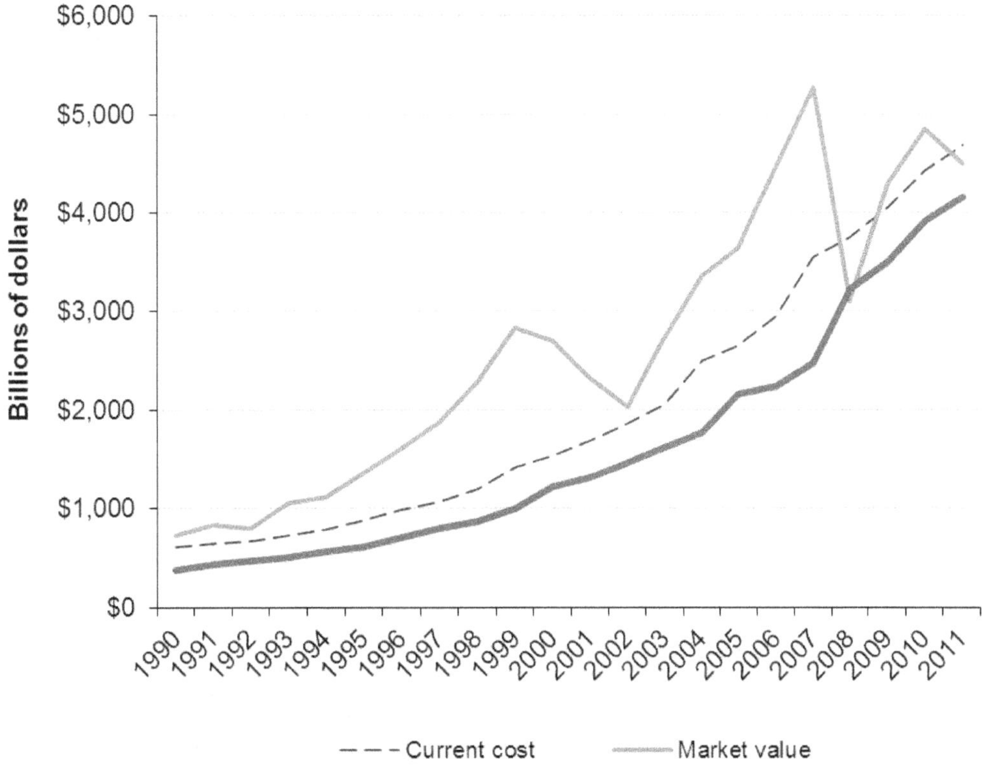

Source: Department of Commerce.

**Figure 2. Foreign Direct Investment in the United States:
Estimated Value of Accumulated Position, 1990-2011**

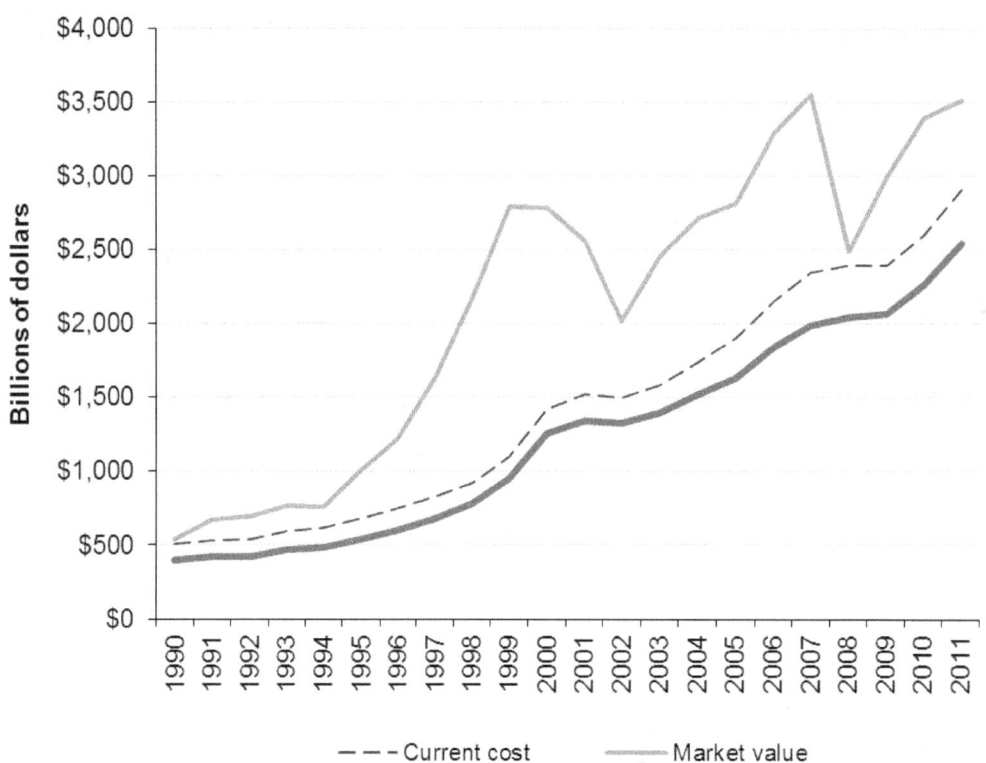

Source: Department of Commerce.

Investment Patterns

Foreign direct investment in U.S. businesses surged in the mid-1980s and has at times outpaced the annual amount of U.S. direct investment abroad. For various reasons, U.S. direct investment abroad and foreign direct investment in the United States have tended to track together so that the annual flows increase or decrease somewhat in tandem,[3] except in 2005, when U.S. direct investment abroad dropped sharply as U.S. parent firms reduced the amount of reinvested earnings going to their foreign affiliates for distribution to the U.S. parent firms in order to take advantage of one-time tax provisions in the American Jobs Creation Act of 2004 (P.L. 108-357). From 2002 and 2004, and again in 2006 to 2011, U.S. direct investment outflows were greater than similar inflows. As a whole, however, the total amount of foreign investment in all U.S. assets has been greater than the total amount of U.S. investment abroad, which has tended to push the net U.S. international investment position further into a negative position. This is not the first time in the nation's history that the U.S. net international investment position has been negative.

---

[3] See CRS Report RL32461, *Outsourcing and Insourcing Jobs in the U.S. Economy: Evidence Based on Foreign Investment Data*, by James K. Jackson.

Early in the nation's history, as the United States made the transition from being a developing economy to being a major economic superpower, foreign investment flowed into capital development projects such as railroad and canal construction, which aided the westward expansion and the development of heavy industries. By 1920, foreigners had withdrawn many of their assets from the United States to finance World War I, which turned the United States into a net creditor. This net creditor position grew unabated after World War II and into the 1980s, when large inflows of foreign investment once again turned the nation's net international investment position into a negative.

The U.S. net debtor status continued to grow through the 1990s and into the 2000s, as indicated by **Figure 3**, which shows U.S.-owned assets abroad and foreign-owned assets in the United States with direct investment valued at historical cost. By year-end 2011, U.S. assets abroad are estimated to have reached $20.6 trillion, while foreign owned assets in the United States were nearly $25 trillion, with direct investments valued at historical cost. As a result, the U.S. net international investment position was estimated to be nearly a negative $4.2 trillion, or equivalent to about 28% of U.S. gross domestic product (GDP), marking a substantial increase in the relative size of the net investment debt position over the 1990s, as indicated in **Table 2**. The net investment position worsened by $1.5 trillion during 2011, from $2.7 trillion to $4.7 trillion with direct investment measured at historical cost, due primarily to large capital inflows, a large increase in financial derivatives, and upward price revisions in foreign-owned assets in the United States. According to the two other measures for direct investment—current cost and market value—the net investment position was valued at about negative $4.0 trillion and negative $4.8 trillion, respectively.

Figure 3. U.S.-Owned Assets Abroad and Foreign–Owned Assets in the United States, 1994-2011

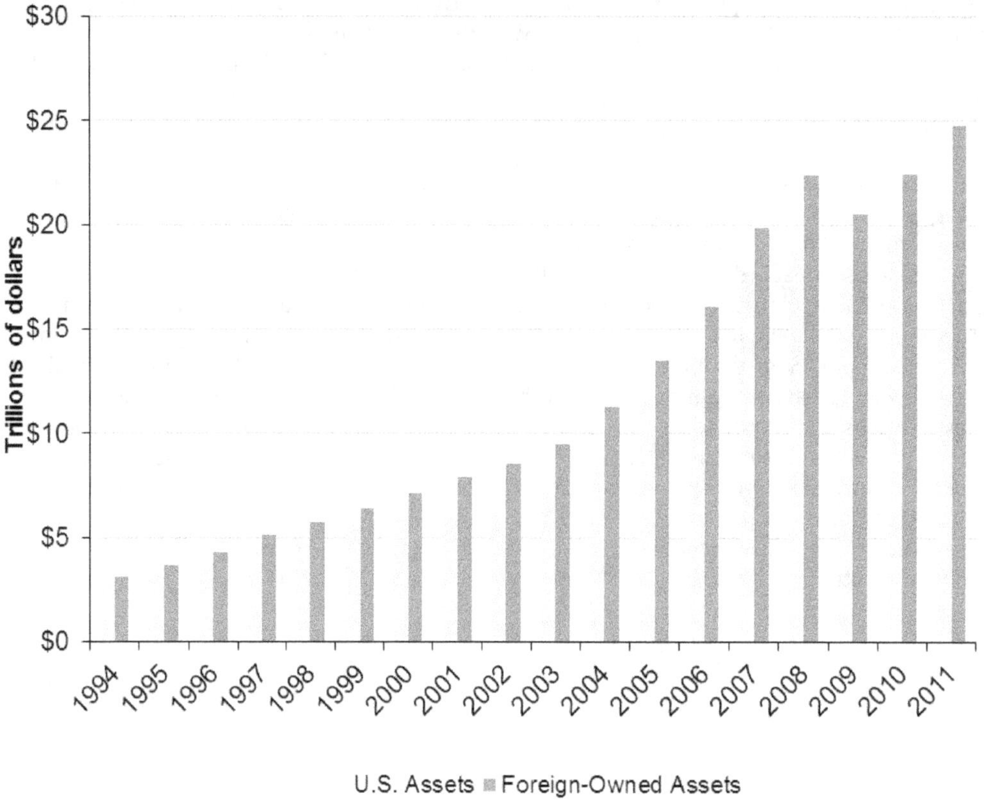

U.S. Assets ■ Foreign-Owned Assets

Source: Department of Commerce.

Table 2. U.S. International Investment Status

(billions of dollars)

	U.S.-Owned Assets Abroad	Foreign-Owned Assets in the United States	U.S. Net International Investment Position	U.S. Gross Domestic Product	Relative Share of U.S. Gross Domestic Product
1980	$541.7	$442.4	$99.4	$2,788.1	3.6%
1985	1,134.5	1,143.0	-8.6	4,217.5	-0.2
1990	1,944.1	2,272.9	-328.8	5,800.5	-5.7
1995	3,213.7	3,717.1	-503.4	7414.7	-6.8
1996	3,741.5	4,285.6	-544.1	7838.5	-6.9
1997	4,295.0	5,128.0	-832.9	8332.4	-10.0
1998	4,770.8	5,715.7	-944.9	8793.5	-10.7
1999	5,560.7	6,382.2	-821.4	9353.5	-8.8

	U.S.-Owned Assets Abroad	Foreign-Owned Assets in the United States	U.S. Net International Investment Position	U.S. Gross Domestic Product	Relative Share of U.S. Gross Domestic Product
2000	5,923.1	7,110.5	-1,187.4	9951.5	-11.9
2001	5,931.8	7,922.1	-1,990.3	10,286.2	-19.3
2002	6,242.4	8,537.7	-2,295.4	10,642.3	-21.6
2003	7,200.2	9,478.1	-2,277.9	11,142.1	-20.4
2004	8,611.8	11,246.1	-2,634.4	11,867.8	-22.2
2005	11,551.5	13,621.8	-2,070.4	12,623.0	-16.4%
2006	13,957.2	16,306.2	-2,349.0	13,377.2	-17.6%
2007	17,840.6	19,842.9	-2,002.4	14,028.7	-14.3%
2008	18,948.7	22,374.1	-3,425.4	14,291.5	-24.0%
2009	18,000.9	20,504.7	-2,503.8	13,939.0	-18.6%
2010	19,782.5	22,438.7	-2,656.2	14,526.5	-18.3%
2011	20,606.4	24,801.7	-4,195.3	15,087.7	-27.8%

Source: Department of Commerce.

The foreign investment position in the United States continues to increase as foreigners acquire additional U.S. assets and as the value of existing assets appreciates. These assets are broadly divided into official and private investments reflecting transactions by governments among themselves and transactions among the public. At times, some observers have been concerned about the amount of foreign official investment in the U.S. economy, particularly in U.S. Treasury securities and, more recently, purchases of U.S. businesses by foreign governments. As **Figure 4** indicates, official asset holdings were valued at about $5.2 trillion in 2011, or about 21% of the total foreign investment position. Official assets include such monetary reserve assets as gold, the reserve position with the International Monetary Fund (IMF), and holdings of foreign currency. An important component of foreign official holdings in the United States is the acquisitions of U.S. Treasury securities by foreign governments. At times, such acquisitions are used by foreign governments, either through coordinated actions or by themselves, to affect the foreign exchange price of the dollar. Foreign currency holdings account for a relatively small share of the total foreign investment position.

**Figure 4. Foreign Official and Private Investment Positions
in the United States, 1994-2011**

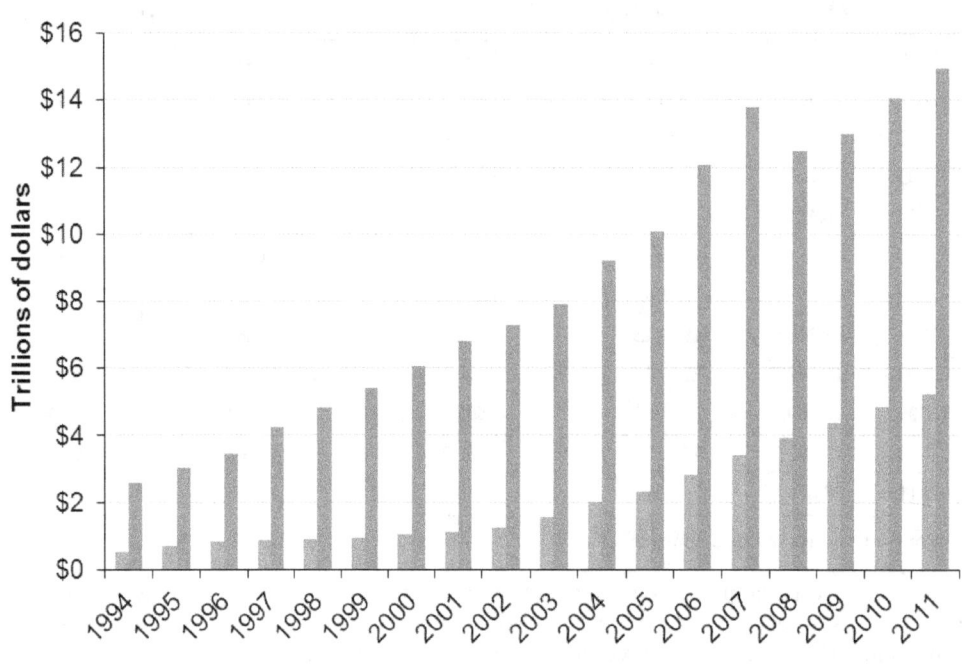

■ Foreign official assets   ■ Private investments

Source: Department of Commerce.

Private asset holdings are comprised primarily of direct investment in businesses and real estate, purchases of publicly traded government securities, and corporate stocks and bonds. Foreign-owned private assets were valued at $15 to $16 trillion, or about 60% of the total foreign-owned assets in the United States. As indicated in **Figure 5**, the composition of U.S. assets abroad and foreign-owned assets in the United States is different in a number of ways. The strength and uniqueness of the U.S. Treasury securities markets make these assets sought after by both official and private foreign investors, whereas U.S. investors hold few foreign government securities. As a result, foreign official assets in the United States far outweigh U.S. official assets abroad. Both foreign private and official investors have been drawn at times to U.S. government securities as a safe haven investment during troubled or unsettled economic conditions, including during the 2008-2009 financial crisis.

Figure 5. U.S. and Foreign Investment Position, By Major Component, 2011

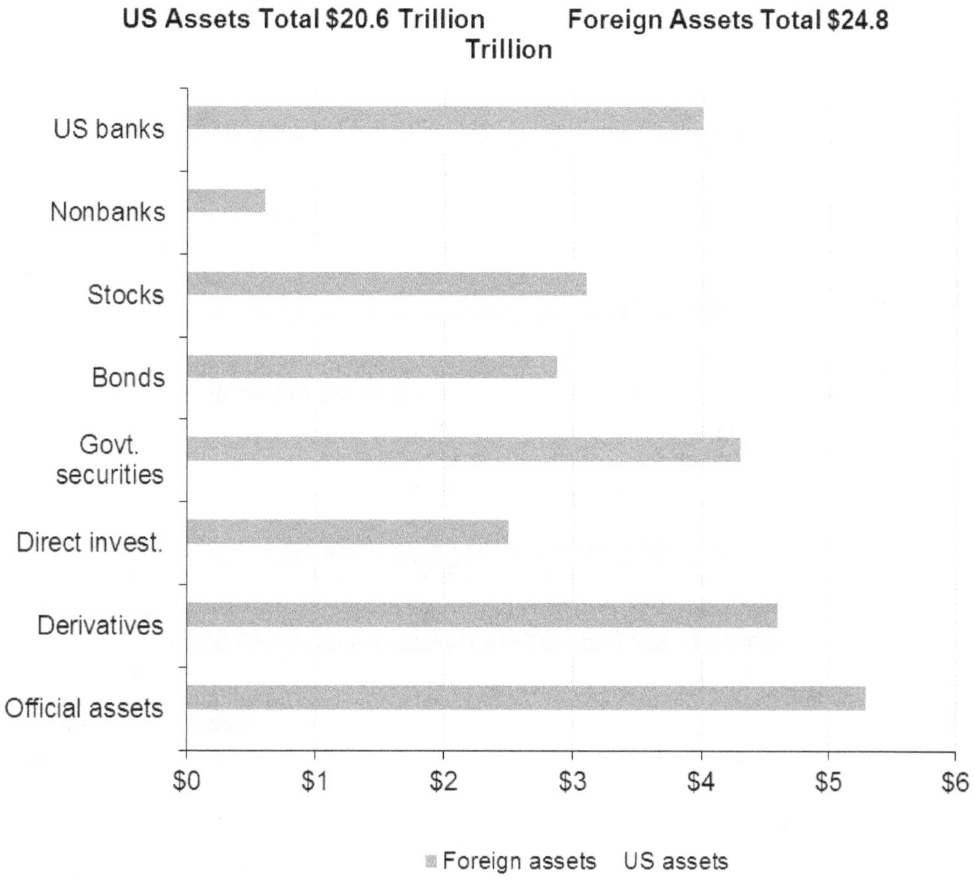

US Assets Total $20.6 Trillion   Foreign Assets Total $24.8 Trillion

■ Foreign assets   US assets

Source: Department of Commerce.

Of all the accounts, inward and outward direct investments are the most closely matched, demonstrating the appeal of such investments to both U.S. and foreign investors. In fact, the United States is unique in that it not only is the largest foreign direct investor in the world, but it is also the largest recipient of direct investment in the world. Foreign investors also have been attracted to U.S. corporate stocks and bonds for the same reasons domestic U.S. investors have invested in them.[4] The decline in the overall value of U.S. corporate stocks after 2000, however, curbed the rate of growth of foreign purchases of these assets. A similar decline in the value of foreign stocks and the depreciation in the value of the U.S. dollar relative to a broad range of currencies reduced the dollar value of American-owned stock holdings abroad. Claims by private banks are also included in the international investment accounts and represent a broad range of international financial transactions, including financing for short-term trade credits associated with exports and imports of merchandise goods.

---

[4] For additional information, see CRS Report RL32462, *Foreign Investment in U.S. Securities*, by James K. Jackson.

International Investment: Sources and Economic Impact

International investment not only has an impact on the U.S. economy, but it is affected by the economy. For U.S. investors, foreign markets provide them with opportunities to seek out the greatest returns for their investments, returns which often are repatriated back to the United States. In addition, U.S. direct investment abroad, for the most part, tends to stimulate U.S. exports, rather than act as a substitute for exports, which in turn stimulates the most productive sectors of the economy.[5] U.S. direct investment abroad is highly sought after by developing countries, which not only want the capital to supplement their own limited domestic sources, but also want American technology and expertise.

Foreign capital inflows augment domestic U.S. sources of capital, which, in turn, keep U.S. interest rates lower than they would be without the foreign capital. Indeed economists generally argue that it is this interplay between the demand for and the supply of credit in the economy that drives the broad inflows and outflows of capital. As U.S. demands for capital outstrip domestic sources of funds, domestic interest rates rise relative to those abroad, which tends to draw capital away from other countries to the United States.

The United States also has benefitted from a surplus of saving over investment in many areas of the world that has provided a supply of funds at low rates of interest. This surplus of saving has been available to the United States because foreigners have remained willing to lend that saving to the United States in the form of acquiring U.S. assets, which have accommodated the growing current account deficits. Prior to the 2008-2009 financial crisis, the United States experienced a decline in its rate of savings and an increase in the rate of domestic investment. The large increase in the nation's current account deficit would not have been possible without the accommodating inflows of foreign capital. Since then, however, the U.S. saving rate increased relative to the prior period and the rate of business investment declined, as indicated in **Table 3**.

As **Table 3** indicates, U.S. saving as a percent of gross domestic product (GDP) is estimated to have increased in 2012 by 0.4% compared with the 2007-2011 period, while investment fell by a slightly larger 0.5% of GDP, so that saving increased as a share of GDP. These changes in the share of saving and investment relative to GDP were accompanied by an increase worldwide in both saving and investment with saving slightly greater than investment, which means there was estimated to be a slight amount of excess saving world-wide in 2012 compared with the 2007-2011 period. Among other advanced economies, both saving and investment in 2012 are estimated to have declined relative to the 2007-2011 period, as a share of GDP, reflecting the slowdown in economic activity in 2011 and 2012. Although saving and investment in the Eurozone and in Japan are estimated to have declined in 2012 relative to the 2007-2011 period, saving continued to be a greater share of GDP, providing additional funds for investment outside those areas. Among the newly industrialized economies in Asia, both saving and investment fell in 2012 relative to the 2007-2011 period, but saving continued to outpace investment as a share of GDP. In the emerging developing economies, the developing economies of Asia (which includes China) experienced a decrease in saving and an increase in investment as a share of GDP, which

---

[5] For additional information, see CRS Report RL32461, *Outsourcing and Insourcing Jobs in the U.S. Economy: Evidence Based on Foreign Investment Data*, by James K. Jackson.

reduced the amount of excess saving provided by the countries in this area. In the Middle East, investment as a share of GDP decreased in 2012 compared with 2007-2011, while saving remained the same, resulting in an increase in the amount of excess saving available for investing elsewhere.

Table 3. Saving and Investment in Selected Countries and Areas; 2007-2011, and 2012

(Percentage of Gross Domestic Product)

Area/Country	Average, 2007-2011	2012	Change
World			
Saving	23.5	24.0	0.5
Investment	23.1	23.9	0.8
United States			
Saving	12.7	13.1	0.4
Investment	16.7	16.2	-0.5
Other Advanced Economies			
Saving	18.8	18.3	-0.5
Investment	19.5	18.8	-0.7
Eurozone			
Saving	20.6	19.9	-0.7
Investment	20.5	18.7	-1.8
Japan			
Saving	24.4	21.9	-2.5
Investment	21.1	20.3	-0.8
Newly Industrialized Asian Economies			
Saving	32.7	31.5	-1.2
Investment	25.9	25.8	-0.1
Emerging Developing Economies			
Saving	33.0	33.3	0.3
Investment	30.5	32.1	1.6
Developing Asia			
Saving	44.0	43.0	-1.0
Investment	40.0	42.1	2.1
Middle East			
Saving	38.3	38.3	0.0
Investment	27.5	26.1	-1.4

Source: *World Economic Outlook*, International Monetary Fund, October 2012. p. 213-214.

Capital inflows also allow the United States to finance its trade deficit, because foreigners are willing to lend to the United States in the form of exchanging the sale of goods, represented by

U.S. imports, for such U.S. assets as stocks, bonds, and U.S. Treasury securities. Such inflows, however, generally put upward pressure on the dollar, which tends to push up the price of U.S. exports relative to its imports and reduce the overall level of exports. Furthermore, foreign investment in the U.S. economy drains off some of the income earned on the foreign-owned assets that otherwise would accrue to the U.S. economy as foreign investors repatriate their earnings back home.

Some observers are particularly concerned about the long-term impact of the U.S. position as a net international investment debtor on the pattern of U.S. international income receipts and payments. In 2011, the United States received $854 billion in income receipts (including receipts on royalties) on its investments abroad and paid out $407 billion in income payments (including payments on royalties) on foreign-owned assets in the United States for a net surplus of $314 billion in income receipts.[6] This surplus has varied over time as changes in interest rates affect payments to foreign investors on such assets as Treasury securities and corporate bonds.[7] As the annual amount of foreign investment in the U.S. economy continues to exceed the amount of U.S. investment abroad, it seems inevitable that U.S. payments on foreign-owned assets will exceed U.S. receipts. A net outflow of income payments would act as a drag on the national economy as U.S. national income is reduced by the net amount of funds that are channeled abroad to foreign investors.

One of the positive areas of the income accounts is the income receipts the United States receives on U.S. direct investments abroad. Although the historical cost values of U.S. direct investment abroad and foreign direct investment in the United States are roughly equal, the United States earned $320 billion more on its direct investment assets abroad in 2011 than foreigners earned on their direct investments in this country, as indicated in **Figure 6**. As indicated previously, in 2005 U.S. parent firms reduced the amount of reinvested earnings going to their foreign affiliates for distribution to the U.S. parent firms in order to take advantage of one-time tax provisions in the American Jobs Creation Act of 2004 (P.L. 108-357).

The performance of foreign-owned establishments, on average, compared with their U.S.-owned counterparts presents a mixed picture. Historically, foreign-owned firms operating in the United States have had lower rates of return, as measured by return on assets, than U.S.-owned firms, although the gap between the two groups appears to have narrowed over time. According to the Bureau of Economic Analysis, this narrowing of the gap in the rate of return appears to be related to age effects, or the costs associated with acquiring or establishing a new business that can entail startup costs that disappear over time and market share.[8] By other measures, foreign-owned manufacturing firms appear to be outperforming their U.S. counterparts.[9]

The U.S. net surplus of income receipts arising from direct investments was offset to a large extent by large net income payments to foreign holders of U.S. government securities, which fell slightly from $140 billion in 2009 to $134 billion in 2011, likely reflecting the low interest rates

---

[6] Scott, Sarah P., U.S. International Transactions: First Quarter of 2012. *Survey of Current Business*, July 2012, p. 59.

[7] Whitehouse, Mark, U.S. Foreign Debt Shows Its Teeth As Rates Climb. *The Wall Street Journal*, September 25, 2006, p. A1.

[8] Mataloni, Raymond J. Jr., An Examination of the Low Rates of Return of Foreign-Owned U.S. Companies, *Survey of Current Business*, March 2000, p. 55.

[9] *Foreign Direct Investment in the United States, Establishment Data for 2002*, Bureau of Economic Analysis, June 2007.

on U.S. treasury securities. The overall U.S. income surplus was increased further by the income payments made to U.S. holders of foreign corporate stocks and bonds. The United States received $254 billion in income from the corporate stocks and bonds Americans owned abroad and paid out $207 billion to foreign holders of U.S. corporate securities, for a net inflow of $47 billion in income receipts on such assets. In addition, the United States received $121 billion in royalties in 2011 on various products and on U.S.-licensed production technology, patents, and copyrighted material. This was over three times the $37 billion the United States paid foreigners in royalties on their investments in the United States.

Figure 6. U.S. Income Receipts and Payments on U.S.-Owned Assets Abroad and on Foreign-Owned Assets in the United States, 2011

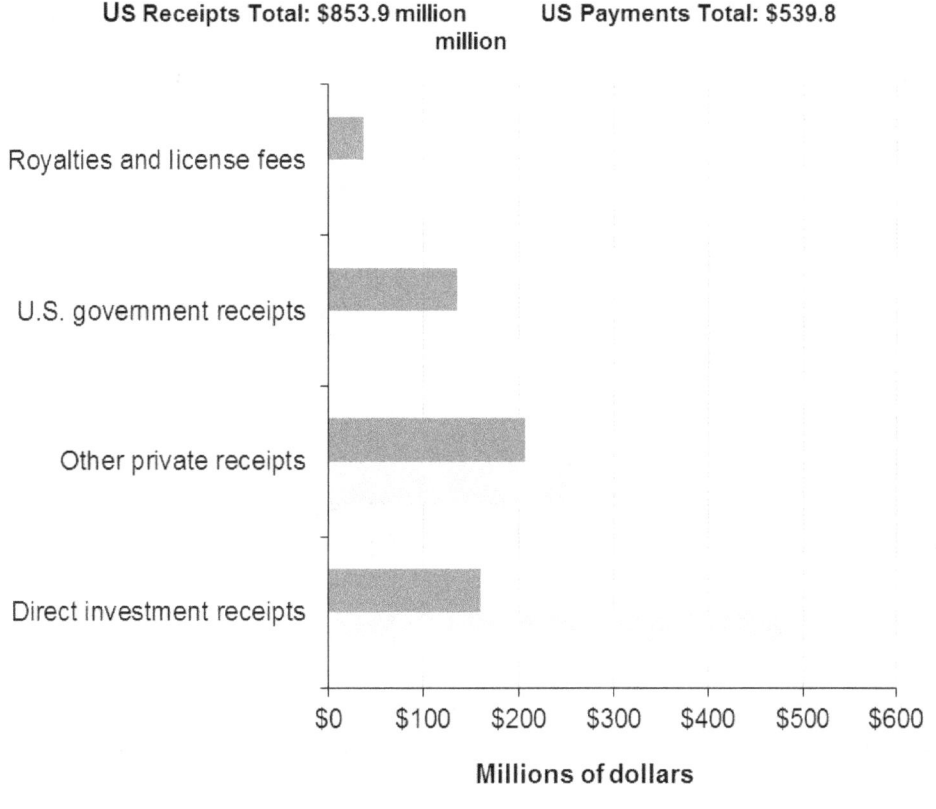

Source: Department of Commerce.

Some observers also are concerned about the extensive amount of foreign investment overall in the U.S. economy and in U.S. financial assets. According to the estimates provided in **Table 4**, foreigners owned approximately 26% of total U.S. wealth in 2011. Although foreign investors own a little more than 7% of total U.S. fixed private capital stock, they own substantially larger shares of U.S. financial assets. For instance, foreign investors now own 50% of total U.S. Federal debt and about half of the outstanding publicly traded U.S. Treasury securities.[10] Some observers argue that such investments could spur an economic crisis in this country should foreign investors decide to pull their money out of the investments, whether for economic or political reasons. This possibility seems remote, however, given the negative impact such an action might have on the foreign investors themselves, but the concerns remain.[11]

Table 4. Estimates of Wealth in the United States, 2011 Current-Cost, Gross Stock Values

(billions of dollars, percent)

Item	Total	Foreign Owned	Foreign Share
Fixed Private Capital	$35,193.20	$2,547.83	7.2%
Nonresidential	$17,632.00	$2,547.83	14.5%
—Agriculture, Forestry, and Fisheries	$515.40	$3.52	0.7%
—Mining	$1,579.20	$136.85	8.7%
—Construction	$273.70	$11.86	4.3%
—Manufacturing	$2,280.30	$838.34	36.8%
—Transportation	$1,131.50	$39.92	3.5%
—Wholesale Trade	$523.20	$309.96	59.2%
—Retail Trade	$1,177.10	$50.55	4.3%
—Finance, Insurance, Real Estate	$1,364.60	$376.77	27.6%
—Services	$3,925.70	$161.14	4.1%
Residential	$17,561.20		
Fixed Government Capital	$11,192.00		
—Equipment	$1,088.80		
—Structures	$9,769.90		
Consumer Durable Goods	$4,732.20		
Financial Assets	$44,818.04	$11,039.40	24.6%
—Federal Debt, Publicly Held	$10,132.04	$5,071.20	50.1%
—Corporate Stocks	$22,824.90	$3,058.20	13.4%
—Corporate Bonds	$11,861.10	$2,910.00	24.5%
—Other		$11,575.39	
Total	$95,935.44	$25,162.62	26.2%

Sources: Nguyen, Elena L., The International Investment Position of the United States at Yearend 2010, *Survey of Current Business*, July 2012. p. 18; Rodriguez, Marilyn, Fixed Assets and Consumer Durable Goods for 2008-2011, *Survey of Current Business*, September 2012. p. 21; Foreign Direct Investment in the United States Tables.

---

[10] For additional information, see CRS Report RL32462, *Foreign Investment in U.S. Securities*, by James K. Jackson.

[11] For a longer presentation of this topic, see CRS Report RL34319, *Foreign Ownership of U.S. Financial Assets: Implications of a Withdrawal*, by James K. Jackson.

Survey of Current Business, September 2012. Table 15; Flow of Funds Accounts of the United States Flows and Outstandings, Second Quarter 2012, Federal Reserve, September, 2012. Tables L212 and L213; Treasury Bulletin, Department of the Treasury, September 2012. Table FD-1.

Congressional Response

Despite expressing concerns at times about the U.S. net international investment position, Members of Congress generally have been reluctant to intervene in the investment process, whether inward or outward. Indeed, successive Congresses and Administrations have led international efforts to eliminate or reduce restraints on the international flow of capital. If the U.S. net investment position continues to turn more negative, prospects increase that the positive U.S. net income receipts will turn negative as U.S. income payments overwhelm U.S. income receipts. In such a case, the U.S. economy will experience a net economic drain as income that could be used to finance new U.S. businesses and investments will be sent abroad to satisfy foreign creditors. Such a drain likely will be small at first relative to the overall size of the economy, but it could grow rapidly if the economy continues to import large amounts of foreign capital.

Some observers are also concerned about the growing role foreign investment is playing in the economy by bridging the gap between domestic sources and demands for credit. One chief consideration is how the capital is being used. Investment funds that are flowing into direct investment and into corporate stocks and bonds presumably are being used to bolster investments in plant and equipment and other investments that aid in corporate productivity over the long run. As such, those investments may well provide a boost to U.S. economic growth well into the future. Foreign investment in U.S. Treasury securities directly aids in financing the federal government's budget deficits and indirectly eases the federal government's demands on domestic credit markets, which assists U.S. firms and consumer consumption by freeing up capital in the economy and by relieving some of the pressure on domestic interest rates.

One growing concern among some policymakers is the rising amount of investment by foreign governments in U.S. businesses, real estate, and portfolio assets (corporate stocks and bonds, and U.S. government securities). Such investments by foreign governments are bolstered by the growing holdings of U.S. currency by foreign governments, known as sovereign wealth funds, which are estimated to amount to more than $2.5 trillion.[12] U.S. policy toward foreign investment generally has been one of acceptance and openness. Investments by foreign governments, however, are viewed by some as a new and different kind of investment that bears greater scrutiny. Such investments by foreign governments are viewed by some as contrary to long-standing U.S. policies which have encouraged foreign governments to shift away from owning businesses enterprises and to support private ownership. For some observers, investments by foreign governments also raise the potential for official interference into a broad range of market activities. There is no evidence to date that ownership of various U.S. assets by foreign governments, by itself, has affected the management of those assets or the markets in which they exist in ways that differ from ownership by private foreign entities. Nevertheless, such concerns likely helped motivate Congress to pass, and President Bush to sign on July 26, 2007, P.L. 110-49, the Foreign Investment and National Security Act of 2007, which increased congressional oversight over acquisitions of U.S. businesses by foreign governments.

---

[12] Weisman, Steven R., A Fear of Foreign Investments. *The New York Times*, August 21, 2007.

Some observers contend that a sharp decline in capital inflows or a sudden withdrawal of foreign capital from the economy could spark a financial crisis. Congress likely would find itself embroiled in any such financial crisis through its direct role in conducting fiscal policy and in its indirect role in the conduct of monetary policy through its supervisory responsibility over the Federal Reserve. Such a coordinated withdrawal seems highly unlikely, particularly since the vast majority of the investors are private entities that presumably would find it difficult to coordinate a withdrawal. Short of a financial crisis, events that cause foreign investors to curtail or limit their purchases of U.S. securities likely would complicate efforts to finance budget deficits in the current environment without such foreign actions having an impact on U.S. interest rates, domestic investment, and long-term rate of growth.

Author Contact Information

James K. Jackson
Specialist in International Trade and Finance
jjackson@crs.loc.gov, 7-7751